EASY MAGIC TRICKS

AMAZING TRICKS WITH EVERYDAY STUFF

by Steve Charney

CAPSTONE PRESS
a capstone imprint

First Facts is published by Capstone Press,
151 Good Counsel Drive, P.O. Box 669, Mankato, Minnesota 56002.
www.capstonepub.com

032010
005740CGF10

 Books published by Capstone Press are manufactured with paper
containing at least 10 percent post-consumer waste.

Library of Congress Cataloging-in-Publication Data
Charney, Steve.
Amazing tricks with everyday stuff / by Steve Charney.
    p. cm. — (First facts. Easy magic tricks)
 Includes bibliographical references and index.
 Summary: "Step-by-step instructions and photos describe how to perform magic
tricks with everyday items"—Provided by publisher.
 ISBN 978-1-4296-4517-1 (library binding)
 1. Magic tricks—Juvenile literature. I. Title. II. Series.
 GV1548.C425 2011
 793.8—dc22   2010003663

Editorial Credits
Kathryn Clay, editor; Matt Bruning, designer; Marcy Morin, scheduler;
  Sarah Schuette, photo stylist; Eric Manske, production specialist

Photo Credits
All photos by Capstone Press/Karon Dubke, except Ed Hord, 24

TABLE OF CONTENTS

INTRODUCTION

Bananas, balloons, and lollipops seem ordinary. But they can be used to perform magic. The **props** in this book are everyday items found around your house (unless you live in a cave).

To keep the **audience** entertained, use **patter** when you perform. Patter can be a joke, a story, or a burp. Just use your imagination to come up with words or noises to make a trick fun.

Remember to practice, practice, practice. Messing up on stage would be worse than failing a math quiz. And practicing is a lot like studying for math. The more you do it, the better you get.

prop—an item used by a performer during a show

audience—people who watch or listen to a play, movie, or show

patter—fast talk used by a magician while performing

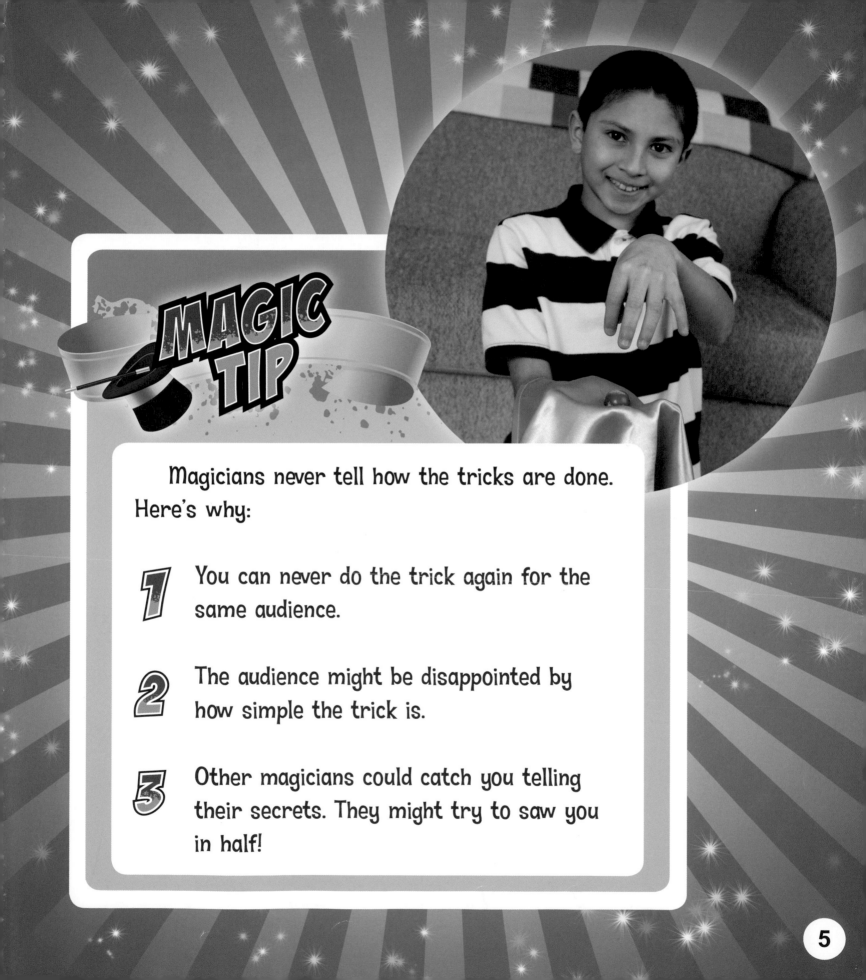

MAGIC TIP

Magicians never tell how the tricks are done. Here's why:

1 You can never do the trick again for the same audience.

2 The audience might be disappointed by how simple the trick is.

3 Other magicians could catch you telling their secrets. They might try to saw you in half!

LOONY BALLOONY

Poke two pins into a balloon. It won't pop! But if you listen closely, you might hear it say "ouch."

Materials: clear tape, a balloon, and two straight pins

Getting Ready:

Place two small pieces of tape near the top of a balloon.

The Trick:

1 Hold the balloon with the tape toward you so your friend can't see it.

2 One at a time, poke the pins into the tape. The balloon doesn't pop.

3 Take out the pins and hold one in your hand. To end the trick with a bang, use the pin to pop the balloon.

MAGIC TIP

Don't blow up the balloon too full. A balloon with too much air is more likely to pop when poked with pins.

THE TIPSY SODA CAN

Blow your friends away by standing a soda can on its edge. Maybe tomorrow you'll make a milk carton do a backflip.

Materials: a soda can one-third full

• • • • Getting Ready:

Drink two-thirds of the soda in a can.

The Trick:

1

Say, "I've trained my soda can to be a gymnast. Watch!"

2

Tip the can until it balances on its edge.

3

Grab the soda and drink a few gulps. If you drink it all, the can will no longer balance.

MAGIC TIP

You can also use an old soda can. Just fill the can one-third full with water.

THE DISAPPEARING TOOTHPICK

Toothpicks are strange. Sometimes they disappear. But then if you wait, they reappear. How strange!

Materials: clear tape and a toothpick

Getting Ready:

Tape the end of a toothpick to your left thumbnail.

The Trick:

1

Make a fist so your thumb is inside your fingers. The toothpick sticks up out of your fist. Your fingers hide your thumbnail and the tape.

Wave your right hand over the left. Say the magic words, "Hocus Jokus."

Open your hand suddenly. Your palm is facing your friend. Your thumb hides the toothpick. The toothpick has disappeared!

Reach into the air like you're grabbing for something. Close your fist. The toothpick has appeared again.

KARATE FINGER

Tell your friend you've been working out. Now you can karate chop a hole straight through a sugar packet with just your finger.

Materials: two sugar packets

• • • • • • • **Getting Ready:**

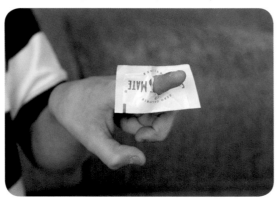

Poke your left index finger through the center of one of the packets. Hide your hand under a table.

• • • • • • • **The Trick:**

Say, "I know finger karate. Watch!" With your right hand, throw the second sugar packet in the air.

2

Catch the packet with your left hand. Use an **overhand** grab.

3

As you catch the packet, hold up your left index finger. It looks like you poked a hole through the second packet.

4

The packet you threw is now hiding in your palm.

overhand—done with your arm raised above your shoulder

MAGIC TIP

If you're standing, hide the first sugar packet by your side. If you're sitting, hide it in your lap.

DON'T WORRY, BE HAPPY

Abraham Lincoln goes from a frown to a smile on a $5 bill. Watch your friend suddenly smile too!

Materials: a crisp $5 bill

• • • • • • • • The Trick:

1

Hold the bill in front of your friend. Say, "Poor Abe Lincoln doesn't know if he's sad or happy. First he's frowning. Then he's smiling."

2

Fold the bill down the center of Lincoln's left eye.

3 Fold the bill down the center of the right eye.

4 Bring the two folds together and fold again.

5 Tip the bill down to show a frowning Lincoln.

6 Now tip the bill up. Lincoln is smiling. Say, "Ah, that's better!"

MAGIC TIP

This trick can be performed using any paper money. Try it with a $1 bill or a $10 bill.

A BANANA FOR TWO

This banana looks ordinary. But you'll want to share it with a friend. Why else would it be cut in half?

Materials: a clean sewing needle, a banana, and a marker

Getting Ready:

Poke a needle into the middle of a banana. Wiggle the needle from side to side. This will slice the banana in two.

Write the number 2 on the banana with a marker.

The Trick:

1

Ask your friend if he's ever seen a presliced banana. Point to the 2 and say that's how many pieces there are.

2

Peel the banana.

3

Show your friend the two pieces. Say, "I don't know how they do it. But it sure tastes good." Offer him a piece.

LOLLI—POP!

Ever wonder how people came up with the word lollipop?
The lolli part is still a mystery, but here's how to get the pop!

Materials: a rubber band, a lollipop, and a paper lunch bag

Getting Ready:

Put a rubber band on your wrist. Tuck the lollipop in the rubber band. Wear a long-sleeved shirt to help hide the lollipop. Open a paper bag. Then fold down the top.

The Trick:

Tell your friend there's a lollipop in the bag. Have her take a look. She sees the bag is empty.

2 Take the bag back and blow it up.

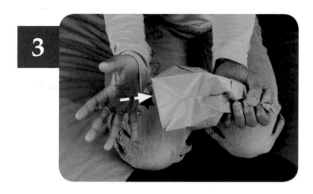

3 Say, "Well, there's no lolli, but here's the POP!" Hit the bag with a loud pop.

4 Secretly grab the lollipop from your wristband. The bag hides the move. It looks like the lollipop magically appeared from inside the bag.

5 Hand the lollipop to your friend.

HAVING A BALL

A ball disappears. Just like that! Suddenly, it's there again. Just like that! And now you're the kid who can perform wonders. Just like that!

Materials: a cloth, a small ball, and a **shill**

· · · · · · · Getting Ready:

Find a friend to be your shill. Explain what he has to do.

· · · · · · · The Trick:

Place a cloth over a ball.

shill

Have the audience feel the ball under the cloth. The last one to reach under the cloth is your shill. He secretly **palms** the ball and takes it away.

shill—someone who pretends to be part of the audience to secretly help you perform a trick

palm—to hide something in your hand

Say, "Abracapocus!" Open up the cloth. The ball is gone! Have people look at the cloth and your hands.

Hold up the cloth. Tell the audience the ball has returned. Have the shill feel it first. He secretly places the ball under the cloth.

Have the other people reach under the cloth. They will feel the ball.

Open up the cloth, and show the ball. The shill should act as surprised as the audience.

GLOSSARY

audience (AW-dee-uhns)—people who watch or listen to a play, movie, or show

imagination (i-MAJ-uh-NAY-shuhn)—the ability to create new images or ideas of things you have never experienced

magician (ma-JI-shuhn)—a person who performs magic tricks

ordinary (ORD-uh-ner-ee)—commonly used or usual

overhand (OH-vur-hand)—done with your arm raised above your shoulder, as in an overhand pitch

palm (PALM)—to hide something in your hand

patter (PAT-ur)—fast talk used by a magician while performing

prop (PROP)—an item used by a performer during a show

shill (SHILL)—someone who pretends to be part of the audience to secretly help you perform a trick

READ MORE

Becker, Helaine. *Magic up Your Sleeve: Amazing Illusions, Tricks, and Science Facts You'll Never Believe*. Berkeley, Calif: Owlkids, 2010.

Charney, Steve. *Hocus-Jokus: How to Do Funny Magic*. Minnetonka, Minn.: Meadowbrook Press, 2003.

Fullman, Joe. *Sleight of Hand*. Magic Handbook. Laguna Hills, Calif.: QEB Pub., 2008.

INTERNET SITES

FactHound offers a safe, fun way to find Internet sites related to this book. All of the sites on FactHound have been researched by our staff.

Here's all you do:

Visit *www.facthound.com*

Type in this code: 9781429645171

INDEX

ABOUT THE AUTHOR

Steve Charney learned magic when he was a little kid. Now he performs more than 100 times each year.

Steve's also a ventriloquist, radio personality, musician, and songwriter. He has written songbooks, storybooks, joke books, and magic books. Look for him on the Internet.